MW00748422

Homeschooling, simplified:
Great Books to study
Canadian History
a guide to studying Canadian history
through historical fiction

Great Books to study Canadian History
a guide to studying Canadian history
through historical fiction
Bonnie Landry
copyright 2004

Dedicated to my husband, Albert
for his encouragement and enthusiasm
and to our children
Breann, Lucy, Mary, Isaac,
Noah, Abel and little Lydia
for teaching me how to read.

Special thanks to family and friends
who helped with reading,
reviewing and editing this book,
to Carolyn Hatcher,
author of "Let the Authors Speak"
for a great way to organize information;
and to St. Thomas Aquinas.

Also, much gratitude to the patient staff at the
South Cowichan Library.

TABLE OF CONTENTS

INTRODUCTION

The goal of this book is to aid homeschooling families in the study of Canadian history. It is written to provide a list of children's literature that families can choose for the purpose of studying Canadian history, and to provide some ideas and resources for studying through literature. Good historical fiction is an excellent way to whet a child's appetite for history.

The impetus for this revision is twofold. My life has changed a lot in thirteen years. Four of our children have graduated and moved on. Their education was "successful" in the sense that they are good people, well rounded, able to think for themselves, and go on to college and university well prepared. Our youngest is nine, and as such, I am finding a little more time to write.

LESSONS IN LITERATURE

Does it work? How has the literary approach to home education played out? Literature as a basis for education, in terms of studying history, geography and all aspects of literature study has produced eager learners. When we set out to homeschool our children one of our goals was that they would love to learn. They do love to learn, and actively pursue educating themselves in many different ways in their lives. It feels like a beautiful thing to see that it "worked."

CANADIAN HISTORY

The success of colonizing and settling Canada was due to the perseverance of early missionaries, explorers and adventurers. For many, the sense of adventure and a better life called them to pursue a life in the New World. For others, their perseverance of creating a new life in a new land was the outpouring of their faith, their love for God and desire to do His will. Still others were driven by greed and power; we will meet them here also.

The books listed in Chapter Four are books that portray the challenges, the events, the politics, and the lives and works of significant people who influenced this developing nation. Many of the books are recommended because they are fine examples of virtue. Many of these books are neutral, in the sense that they do not make a comment on whether or not people's actions were morally right or wrong. Books such as these can be valuable for relaying history, but most parents would like to know which books encourage training in virtue as well. Books that glorify vice have been avoided. For example, if the protagonist in a story pursues revenge, and revenge becomes an attractive quality to emulate, the book is not appropriate for young readers. There are many heroes in Canadian history; there are also villains. Through literature we are given an opportunity to see the grace that comes through virtuous action, such as courage, charity, perseverance and wisdom, and the consequences of vice. Books that illuminate the ideals we want to present to our children are an important part of our day.

There are many worthy books written about Canadian history. Many are out of print, or have been around long enough to be considered passé. This list of books, ordered chronologically, have benefited our family, and may benefit others who want to study Canadian history through literature, or supplement their history program. Most parents start choosing literature for historical studies through homeschool catalogues. This is a good place to start, as most homeschool suppliers are home educating parents themselves, and provide some of the best children's literature available on Canadian history. Many of the newer books I have not included, as descriptions and review of these newer books are already accessible to parents. I have included a few books available in homeschool catalogues when it would be a loss to *not* include them in Canadian history studies. In homeschool catalogues, however, we don't have access to many older books.

I started looking for older and out of print historical fiction. The more I looked, the more I found, so I started doing some serious digging (and serious reading). The more I read, the more I wanted to read. Canadian history is by no means dull. The result is nearly 200 books listed here. A short description of each book is provided. Every effort has been made to provide a selection of books for each event or particular period in Canadian history, however, some periods of history have been much more appealing for authors to write about, such as pioneers and the Gold Rush; some topics, then, have several books to choose from, others just a few.

The books listed have a key, labelling them fiction, or non-fiction and the approximate reading level. Few people would have time to read all these books in a study of Canadian history. If you are studying together as a family, nothing beats reading aloud. Reading together provides the common backdrop for what to study, and children can choose other books from the main list, or parents can choose for them.

A short comment needs to be made about "political correctness." Many of the books listed would be considered politically incorrect. Not because they treat any particular group of people with disdain or disrespect, but because in the

1940's, 1950's or 1960's, when many of these books were written, the authors did not know that the language and terms they used would change, and the words they were using would one day be considered condescending or a racial slur. In many of the books the First Nations people of Canada are referred to as natives, Indians, heathens, and occasionally even "savages." References such as these used today would be crass, but considering that the term "First Nations" was not yet in use, we need to take the books for what they are. What is far more significant is how the author treats his subject, and how he presents justice and injustice done to all people throughout Canada's history.

Chapter One
Studying Canadian History Through Literature

Why study Canadian history through literature? Most approaches to home education stress the importance of good literature. Classical education, "Great Books," Charlotte Mason, unschooling... whatever approach is taken to educate children, most families who have a high regard for education provide their children with good books to read; they value literacy as an important asset. Most parents learn right from the start that children love books; they love to be read to, and that history comes alive through historical fiction. This book includes some thoughts on studying history through literature, ideas for how to approach history, as well as commentary on including Canadian material when the curriculum chosen is predominantly American. The main intent, however, is to provide a timeline of literature to study Canadian history.

BOOK GUIDES

There are several excellent books published which help families choose good literature for their children's education. Three book guides that I have used extensively, and are classics on the home education bookshelf are: *Honey for a Child's Heart* by Gladys Hunt, *Books Children Love* by Elizabeth Wilson, and *Let the Authors Speak* by Carolyn Hatcher. An excellent book to discern good literature is *A Landscape With Dragons* by Michael O'Brien. It also includes a reading list. *Designing Your Own Classical Curriculum* by Laura Berquist and Susan Shaeffer McAuley's *For the Children's Sake*, are both books that stress the vital importance of what our children are fed. They are recommended reading for not just home educating parents, but all parents.

ENCYCLOPEDIAS

A decent set of encyclopedias is vital for instant access to topics that you want to know more about when reading historical fiction. Encyclopedias are the most direct route to information when you want to take advantage of the "teachable moment." We use *World Book*, as the format is appealing and accessible. Relatively inexpensive from used bookstores, local or online versions, World Book will still contain much accurate information even if it is ten or twenty years old. World Book is sold new online. Purchasing "last year's" model, or sometimes even the year before is a huge savings. They are brand new encyclopedias and half the price or less.

Most libraries update their World Book each year or two, so if recent information is required for older students (such as the accuracy of Canadian economic statistics or political issues), you can access that information from an up-to-date source. If your child wants to know more about the War of 1812 when the book you are reading refers to it, an encyclopedia is going to be the easiest, and more importantly, the quickest, way of getting that information. If you tell your child that you'll go to the library tomorrow and find some good books on the War of 1812, or you'll research it together later, the pertinence of the information at the moment is likely to be lost.

ENCYCLOPEDIAS ONLINE

Is an online version of an encyclopedia a better alternative to "real" encyclopedias? This, of course, is a subjective and biased comment, but there is truth in it; it is difficult to snuggle around a computer. You can however, have three or four children cuddled up with you on the couch looking up something interesting. We spend *hours* with encyclopedias, when one topic leads to another... and another, there are often several encyclopedias spread out on the table, and information being passed back and forth readily.

This is not to say that online encyclopedias have no place in learning. There are some fun and interesting interactive aspects to online learning tools. Also, if you subscribe to an online encyclopedia, you will always have the most up to date information on areas such as politics and science and technology. Particularly for high school students, this information is important, but it is also available at your local library. Computer encyclopedias are an excellent complement, but can't really take the place of a real book, can they?

And here's another thought on entering into the World Wide Web of information. We all know that the instant we open a website, we are enticed to go down a lot of little rabbit trails. Our brains become pretty absorbed quickly into "another world." We see this in our kids, too. It's so easy to while away our time once we enter that world. So why not capitalization on that natural inclination? Why not find the excellent and exciting and relevant websites that you want to use, and present those to your kids? To enhance what you are learning about together. Enter that other world for a little while. Go on an inexpensive field trip with your kids for the afternoon! The efficient and appropriate use of computers in education can to be valuable. Avoiding the negatives (time wasting, rabbit trails) and work with the best the Internet has to offer with a little planning. In the resources of this book, there are some great websites listed to help you along the way.

TYING HISTORY TOGETHER

It's important to tie Canadian history together in sequence so that it makes sense. There are a few ways of doing this, and probably using a history book or text with a timeline is the most effective way. World Book can be used for this purpose; the article on Canadian history is excellent, and suitable for middle grade students and high school students. Another option for middle grades would be Donalda Dickie's book *My First History of Canada* (2), updated by Rudi Krause. This is a lovely brief chronology of Canadian history; not too much detail is given on each topic, but it is a short, pithy outline of Canadian history. Discussion questions after each chapter may be used for discussion, writing and research topics. Warmly written and often humorous, our family has enjoyed this book thoroughly. Another book we have enjoyed is an out of print book called *The Story of Canada* by Isabel Barclay. It is written at an almost story book level, to bring younger children into the study of Canada.

Arranged partly chronologically and partly thematically, the newer book by Janet Lunn also by the title *The Story of Canada* is a valuable complement to Canadian history. This is a large "coffee table" book that is nicely written, and visually appealing. Not to be used as a text per se, but a lovely addition to Canadian history as a whole, and particularly useful to families teaching with children at different ages, as it is so visually appealing.

TIMELINES

Timelines are an effective way of tying history together so it all makes sense. A timeline book can be made as you go along studying Canadian history. A simple timeline can be posted on the wall to show the broad categories of Canadian history, or a more detailed timeline can be used to show the many events and people that made this country. A combination of all three is the best approach.

Other sources through which Canadian history can be studied are poetry, folk music particular to our history, and painters who have captured history through their artwork. A selection of poetry and some of the most significant artists in Canadian history are included in Chapter Seven. A short selection of poetry has been chosen to reflect some aspect of Canadian history; the titles of these poems are listed with the booklist chronologically. The poems included are in the public domain, so they are reprinted here, but here is an exhaustive archive available through a federal web site, the National Poetry Archive (see resources chapter). There is huge list of Canadian poets and their works.

FINDING RESOURCES

Much of the literature listed in this book is out of print but it will be available from local libraries. Library inventories vary from place to place, but most libraries offer an interlibrary loan service for books they do not stock. In the resources chapter of this book, there are listed some excellent websites for used booksellers.

We have used the book *Let the Authors Speak* to choose books for historical studies. Because our family studies history through literature, this book has been an incredible gift to me. All books are listed in it chronologically; reference books, fiction, non-fiction, and books that were written during a particular era. Many of the books Mrs. Hatcher lists however are out of print or difficult to find.

The process we take to find books we want to read is that we check for it first in home education catalogues, then we check the local library. If it isn't there, we search the interlibrary loan system, and we almost always find the book we are looking for. Then, (like most book lovers) if we really enjoy the book, we buy it. First I check the local bookstore, and they research the book on their database. If it comes up as out of print, and unavailable, I start checking used booksellers online.

The list of Canadian books and resources provided is not exhaustive. It represents some of what many parents consider the best resources available, the ones that work well together, and those I have found most efficacious in teaching my own children. A great deal of time was spent on the books listed here: some were found by intentional digging, others stumbled over by Divine Providence. Please feel free to contact me if you have come across resources that you consider an asset to revisions that may be made to this book. Contact information is in Chapter Eight: Resources.

Chapter Two
How a Book Becomes the Curriculum

APPROACHES TO STUDYING HISTORY

Virtually all of Canadian history, like most history, can be studied through good literature. The approach our family takes to studying history and geography is through historical fiction. In this chapter, I'll be laying out our approach for doing this. Many people prefer to study history through a textbook or program approach, and then use historical fiction to supplement their program. These suggestions can be used to supplement any Canadian history program.

HOW TO READ A BOOK

I like to choose several books that we will read out loud as a family; read aloud book always becomes the main theme for what we study. I provide other books that my children can choose to read on their own. This draws in the whole family. Children rarely tire of being read to. We use a piece of loose-leaf paper folded in half lengthwise as a book mark, and as things come up that we want to know more about, I jot them down. After reading a chapter or two, we start looking up the things we noted such as new words, ideas or places. Anything of interest that we want to look up in the encyclopedia or other resource book is written down; for example, if we were reading *Madeleine Takes Command* we might note forts and their structure and purpose, the Mohawks, The St. Lawrence River, New France, Montreal, Quebec and Three Rivers. We might also look up what kind of canoes were used then, how they were made and what they were made of, or muskets and how they worked.

If we were reading **The Story of Rolf and the Viking Bow** we could research Iceland, Norse mythology and sagas, Viking tools, weapons and lifestyle. It would depend on what took our interest as we were reading, or what I wanted my children to know about. Younger children typically find information on the culture more interesting and accessible. Food, clothing, modes of transportation, weapons and recreation are usually what children start out wanting to know. These make good topics to write about at younger ages. As they mature, they are ready to understand more about politics, conflict and the development of ideas. Discussing these ideas are what moves a child into essay writing from "report" writing.

DEVELOPING AN OUTLINE FOR STUDY

If you are concerned that they are not covering Everything That Needs to be Covered, relax. There is a seldom-used resource in World Book that is a huge benefit to homeschoolers. This is the Research Guide. Very last in the collection you receive with a full set of World Book, this resource and study guide is set up so that a topic may be looked up, and then every World Book article containing information on that topic is listed. The outline in the Research Guide can be used as an outline for parents to plan what they want to study. For example, under the heading "Canada, History of" you will find a list like the following:

Canada, History of   C: 140
    Civil Rights (Civil Rights in Canada)   **Ci: 610**
    Confederation of Canada   **Ci: 932**
    Franklin, Benjamin
    (A delegate in London) **F: 490**
    Fur Trade   **F: 565**
    (and so the list goes alphabetically)

There are several other listings under this heading, as well as a note referring to the "related articles" listed at the end of the History of Canada article. There are several other headings for Canada as well, such as:

Canada,
Government of Canada,
Dominion of Canada,
Federal Court of Canada;

and many others.

A direct copy of the headings in the Research Guide can be used as an outline to a Canadian History study, or the headings can be used to develop an outline. Any general book on Canadian history, like *My First History of Canada* or the *Story of Canada*, also have tables of contents. Those can be used as your outline as well. Photocopy the outline, and keep it handy. Tick off anything you have read, talked about or studied. Cross off anything you won't be covering this time around.

HOW TO FORCE KIDS TO LEARN STUFF YOU THINK THEY SHOULD KNOW

Whether you use a program for the study of history or not, the question burning on most parents minds at this point is: "But how do I force them to learn stuff I think they should know?" Two successful methods can be used for this. I call them "salting the oats" and "flooding." Salting the oats, as you might guess, is simply asking a few leading questions, or going on a field trip pertaining to the subject you're broaching, or picking up a new book on the topic. Best bet not to announce that you just bought (or got from the library) a lovely book about Vikings that you are going to read, if that's the subject your children are balking at. Best to just leave it lying around, perhaps even still in the bag. Make it a really great "Eyewitness Book" or something equally appealing. Flooding requires a trip to the library. Pick up every book you can find on the topic, and DVDS, too if you like. Their curiosity will get the better of them. If the little children ask you to read one of them out loud, be sure to do it; older children will inevitably perk up their ears.

Occasionally it takes a little more effort. Some kids will study anything that has to do with animals. So let them start there. "What animals are in Ontario, let's put them on a map. Oh look, I bet those deer drank right out of this river off the St. Lawrence that Samuel de Champlain sailed down. I bet they stood right there watching him build his fort." I'm sure you get the idea. Flooding is best done before you read any novel that has a particular focus--Explorers, Vikings, Inuit, the

War of 1812... any topic can be flooded. Tailor your study to your child's interest. If you have a child interested only in reading biographies, Canadian history could predominantly be studied through reading about the lives of its influential people, connected together logically through a timeline.

MULTI-AGE TEACHING

If you are teaching several different age ranges together at one time, don't be concerned that a book or encyclopedia article you are reading may be too advanced for the younger ones. They will take what they can, and when they are saturated with information, they will walk away. When they are older, and you study Canadian history again, they will take in what they can at that age. On the topic of reading to several ages at once; let the little ones play with play dough or eat their lunch or do Lego to keep their little fingers busy while you read. They will be less disruptive, and will likely absorb more of what you are reading because they are busy and quiet.

It takes less energy to think of and provide a small activity at reading time than it does to try and talk over them, or keep little ones quiet. On the other hand, some children *need* to be physical or turn cartwheels in order to assimilate what you are reading. Even bigger kids like to draw, crochet or do play dough while you read. Older children can take turns reading out loud if you need to attend to smaller ones, or even if you don't need to.

Many suggestions will be made for resources to put up on the wall. Anything you can put up on a wall should be put where it can be easily seen, or it is pointless to have it there. Dealing with toddlers while teaching older children makes this problematic, however.

Here are a couple of ideas to keep charts and posters legible and all in one piece. Maps and charts can be put on a table or desk (the kitchen table is a great place for this, as children seem to spend so much time there, eating, playing play dough, doing crafts, etc.) and then covered by a thick sheet of clear plastic that can be purchased from a fabric store. This plastic can be taped or stapled to the bottom of the table to keep it in place, but if you purchase a heavier weight, it isn't usually necessary.

Alternately, thin stiff plastic can be purchased from plastic shops (they will cut it the right size for your chart or map) and then tacked over the chart with finishing nails. Of course, the easiest option is to buy heavy laminated charts and maps where available if toddlers and small people are around. After about fifteen years of homeschooling my kids, I invested in my ultimate dream table (oh, the dreams of the homeschooling mother!)...I had thick plastic sheets cut the exact size of my tables...now I don't have to replace the plastic tablecloths, and it is super easy to slide stuff underneath. If budget allows, this would be an excellent early investment.

If table space is at a premium, and you want to have a more serene dinner environment as a family, a tablecloth over the plastic sheet and school stuff transforms the room! As a space saver, a family can also develop a binder with binder sized maps, charts or timelines in it, so it can be put away after discussion. If you have a large family, I would recommend having a couple of these binders, so that everyone can see the maps and timelines while you read. One the righthand sidebar of my blog, *oh, that's simple* I have a link to a resource that sells hundreds of binder sized items…Pinterest is a valuable source or printables, too.

MIDDLE GRADES AND HIGH SCHOOL

In the school system, topics are studied more than once throughout the school years. This is true in home education also. Most guides will recommend studying Canadian history one year in the middle grades, and again in high school. Because our family studies history together, I typically use middle grade resources, knowing that younger kids will pick up what they can, and older kids will be supplemented with higher level books and resources. I also include storybooks for the younger children, and chosen well, the older ones enjoy the stories too.

In the middle grades, *My First History of Canada* (2) by Dickie and Krause would make a good backbone. The *World Book* article on Canadian history is another option. Read through one of these first, or several chapters. It would be a good idea to make a simple timeline at this point, making reference to the broad divisions in Canadian history (see timeline chapter). When you begin reading historical fiction, children will have some dates to match up with the information they are getting from other sources including resource books that you have "flooded" and field trips you have taken.

Encyclopedias are fabulous for anything that may come up in the novel you are studying. They are the first point of reference. For example, there will be two or three paragraphs on the War of 1812 in the Canadian history article in World Book. At the end of that introductory article, it will say (see War of 1812). There is an amazing amount of Canadian history available in World Book alone.

As in the younger grades, older children could read through the World Book article first, make a basic timeline from it, and then start choosing literature from each era, to bring history to life. Older kids typically enjoy being read to also; we usually are reading one book aloud, and they are also choosing books from the list provided. It's good to challenge older kids with a few higher level books, but learning happens in an environment of joy, not frustration, so don't push them too far. In fact, frustration will probably just lead to an innate distaste for history, and perhaps even reading. The books on the list provided here were chosen because they would be enjoyable to all ages, one of the hallmarks of good literature.

Chapter Three
General Books about Canadian History

BOOK SERIES

There are a few book series that are worth noting here. The Canadian History Series, edited by Thomas B. Costain is a series of five books, written at an adult level. They would be suitable for an in-depth study of Canadian history for older students, or students who prefer non-fiction history, or for keeners of Canadian history. They would also make good reference books for older high school students. All of these books are written at an adult or advanced reader level, and all are non-fiction. The five books in the series are:

The White and The Gold:

The French Regime in Canada

Century of Conflict:

The Struggle Between the French and British in Colonial America

The Path of Destiny:

Canada From the British Conquest to Home Rule, 1763-1850

From Sea unto Sea:

The Road to Nationhood, 1850-1910

Ordeal by Fire:

Canada, 1910-1945

Virtually every bibliography in any North American history book that I came across, both in fiction and non-fiction, acknowledged the work of Francis Parkman. Parkman is considered to be one of the greatest historians of North America. His particular area of study led him to produce seven volumes describing the struggle for the control of North America, giving a vivid and realistic account of the role played by the native North Americans. All of these books are written at an adult or advanced reader level, and all are non-fiction. Some books by Parkman that may be of interest are:

Pioneers of France in the New World

The Jesuits in North America

The Discovery of the Great West

Montcalm and Wolfe:
The French and Indian War

La Salle and the Discovery of the Great West

The Old Regime in Canada

A notable children's series, "Adventures in Canadian History" by Pierre Berton is widely available through libraries and used bookstores. These are exciting, well-written books for pre-teens; there are several short books in the series, each covering a particular event, aspect or person in Canadian history. We came across an occasional comment that we considered inappropriate for children. The books in this series will be noted. I recommend them, with a suggestion that parents read them first, to determine if they are suitable for their children, or so that the parent can edit as they choose. This series is particularly graphic in its descriptions; however it should be noted here that many of the books listed are written about war, conflict, strife, poverty and hardship. Any parent who has a sensitive child should pre-read these books. The books noted as storybooks, or those that are described as reading level (1) would be suitable for young or sensitive readers.

Although they are non-fiction, many of Berton's "Adventures in Canadian History" books read like a novel. Great Stories of Canada (GSC) is a series of books for children on Canadian history that were published in the sixties. Most of these are works of non-fiction as well, but some read like historical fiction, so they are listed as fiction. There are several books listed from the Buckskin Books series (BB). They are all early reading level, large print novels. Usually based on the true story of a particular person or event, the Buckskin series captures what younger people usually like--lots about the culture, not too much of the politics.

Our family is less likely to enjoy non-fiction books as much for reading aloud, as "information books" are harder to listen to for a longer period of time. The fall and rise of a good plot can keep them listening attentively for much longer. Because of this, the information books or non-fiction usually are among the books that they can choose to read to themselves, alternately I sometimes read them for five minutes or so before we get into the meat of a great novel.

You will probably find that your children are drawn to a certain genre, or author. If they like some books of the Great Stories of Canada series, or a book by Pierre Berton, Barbara Greenwood or Ronald Syme, they will probably like most of the others in that series or by that author.

Some of the books listed are by American authors, a few even by British authors. The objective of this list is to provide readers with a picture of Canadian history through literature, not a list of strictly Canadian literature. Some books are set mainly in the United States or in Europe but provide good background to historical events in and involving Canada, thereby complementing Canadian history studies.

BOOK KEY

The keys used in the book reviews provided in the next section are meant only as an approximate guide as reading levels vary widely. However, it is necessary to provide some kind of guide to the level of the book. Level (1) would be suitable for an early reader, with short chapters and large print, either as a read aloud or for young readers to read on their own. Level (2) would be suitable for a fluent reader or as read aloud choices for younger children; most of these books however, would be enjoyable for all age groups; fiction books in (2) would be particularly good as read aloud books. Level (3) books are adult or advanced readers.

Storybooks vary widely in their reading level, but even when the text is noted as suitable for older children, vivid pictures are a great way of drawing younger children into what the family is studying. After the title of each book in parentheses is "F" for fiction or "NF" for non-fiction. Many of these books, regardless of level, would make good read aloud books for younger children, and older children will enjoy some easier books. The adults who reviewed some of these books enjoyed them. The goal is to access good literature; one of the hallmarks of good literature is that it appeals to all ages.

Chapter Four
A CHRONOLOGICAL LIST
of Canadian Historical Literature

Books marked with an asterisk (*) are suggestions for a core study for approximately grades 7 and up.

Blank space has been left intentionally in each era so that parents can add books and movies that have been good additions to their history study.

Please let me know if you have
books to suggest to add!

Early Canada: Indigenous People

Houses of Snow, Skin and Bones (NF, 1, storybook) by Bonnie Shemie: A short, visual storybook written on two different levels.   At a primary level there is a simple story of dwellings of the Inuit.   An intermediate level portrays the structure of early dwellings, and how the Inuit made them, lived in them, and dealt with the conditions of their habitat.   There are several other books on the same theme by Bonnie Shemie, who shares her fascination with the dwellings of Native people in the woodlands, plains and coastal areas.   They are *Houses of Bark, Houses of Hide and Earth*, and *Houses of Wood*.

Nkwala (F, 2) by Edith Lambert Sharp: Nkwala, a native boy of the Salish tribes of the west coast, is coming of age. He endures much to become a man, and through his story is shown the story of his people and their culture.

*The Whale People** (F, 2-3) by Roderick Haig-Brown: Young Atlin, of the Hotsath people, a West Coasttribe, becomes chief after his father's death. This is an enthralling depiction of the culture and customs of the Whale People.

The Boy and the Buffalo (F, 1, BB) by Kerry Wood: A young native boy is separated from his band during a hunt on the prairie. He spends over a year under the protection of a buffalo herd, and is reunited with his people with this strange story to tell.

Saint Brendan and Vikings

*Into the Ice: The Story of Arctic Exploration
(NF, 1-3) by Lynn Curlee: Written in a fascinating
narrative, this book describes the history of Arctic
exploration. Its artwork is captivating, and it
includes the story of the voyage of St. Brendan in
the 600's A.D. Covering exploration to modern
times, this is a memorable history of the first
encounters with Canada. It reveals some of the
reasons why men continued to pursue the northern
part of the New World despite the harsh
conditions of this frozen land.

Brendan the Navigator (NF, 1) by Jean Fritz: A
short story that discusses the myths, legends and
facts that surround the story of St. Brendan, who
is considered to be possibly the first European to
make a voyage to the New World. If your child is
particularly fascinated with this story, they may
like to have The Brendan Voyage read to them (see
next entry). The postscript to Brendan the
Navigator introduces Tim Severin's research on St.
Brendan.

The Brendan Voyage (3, NF) by Tim Severin:
This is a non-fiction book detailing the journey
taken by Tim Severin, which was a copy of the
journey in the 600's by St. Brendan and his monks
from Ireland to North America. Written at an

adult level, this book could be used as a read aloud. It is a fascinating account of one of the earliest voyages from Europe to Canada. Tim Severin copied both the boat that was used and the journey that was taken. He compares many of his findings on his voyage with the notes taken by St. Brendan, and ultimately surmises that the voyage could have indeed been to North America.

The Kids Book of the Far North (NF, 2) by Ann Love and Jane Drake: A history of Arctic exploration, facts and lore, including a section on the prehistoric Arctic and the impact of the Ice Age. Stories and legends, spirituality of the Northern people discussed.

Beorn the Proud (F, 2) by Madeleine Pollard: A beautifully written novel that looks at the struggle of faith between the pagan practices of the Vikings, and the Christians whose lives the Vikings were ravaging.

*Rolf and the Viking Bow (F, 2) by Allen French: Exquisite saga-type prose tells the story of Rolf and his father, Hiarandi the Unlucky. The tale recounts Rolf's quest to find the bow that will prove his father's innocence.

Leif the Lucky (NF, storybook) by D'Aulaire: This storybook portrays the voyage and adventures of Leif Ericksson. He and his fellow travellers were the first white men to inhabit Canada, 500 years before Columbus. They carry the story of the new land home to their families, where over the years, it becomes a legend.

Nordic Gods and Heroes, and **Children of Odin** (F, 2) by Padraic Colum: The author of these stories captures the qualities and richness of a culture by retelling its tales in exquisite prose. Through Norse mythology, we gain an understanding of what drove the Norsemen, what enticed them here, and what virtues they valued.

Myths of the Norsemen (F, 3) by G.A. Guerber: A collection of Norse mythology, particularly interesting to children who love legends and myths. Written for older children, 12 and up, many of these stories would make good read aloud tales for younger students.

***The Vikings** (F, 2) by Elizabeth Janeway: A novel based on the Norse sagas, depicting the adventures and trials of the Vikings who tried to settle the land they were so drawn to in North America. A rich and authentic tale, beautifully told.

Early Exploration

The World of Columbus and Sons (NF, 2) by Genevieve Foster: This book, and others on Christopher Columbus, give us insight into the initial driving force, and the historical background of men who pursued discoveries of the New World. In particular, the author discusses and introduces us to the world events and personalities that shaped the exploration of the New World.

Columbus (NF, storybook, 1-3) by d' Aulaire: a large picture book biography, encouraging the reader to analyze the life of Columbus. Reveals the fearless nature of one of the most renowned explorers in history, and the brave men who accompanied him.

Columbus: Finder of the New World (F, 1) by Ronald Syme: Like all of Ronald Syme's tales of explorers and adventurers, this is a short, fast moving account. This book details the trials and tribulations of Columbus.

*He Went With Christopher Columbus (F, 2) by Louise Andrews Kent: This book portrays the voyages of Columbus through the eyes of a young boy who travels with him. Columbus' struggle, perseverance and faith make him the young man's hero and mentor.

John Cabot and His Son Sebastian (F, 2) by Ronald Syme: This is a fast paced biography of the life and events of Giovanni Caboto, whose discovery of the Canadian Coast in 1497 almost went ignored, and the life of his son, both shrouded in mystery and historical dispute.

*Cartier Sails the St. Lawrence (F, 2) by Esther Averill: Jacques Cartier makes three expeditions to the New World. "His River", eventually called the St. Lawrence, becomes his great discovery. Based on Cartier's personal journals, the life of the native people, the vast wilderness and the hope that the great river will lead him to China are beautifully related.

Cartier: Finder of the St. Lawrence (F, 1) by Ronald Syme: An excellent short novel that describes the adventures and trials of Jacques Cartier in his excursions down the St. Lawrence.

Cartier Discovers the St. Lawrence (NF, storybook, 1-3) by William Toye: An interesting storybook that details the experiences of Jacques Cartier. Many quotes directly from his journals are included. Suitable for all ages but there is much text written at a higher level.

The Man from St. Malo, the Story of Jacques Cartier (NF, 2, GSC) by Robert Ferguson: This is a lively biographical account of Cartier who claimed Canada for France.

*Jacques Cartier** (poem) by Thomas D'Arcy McGee: a poem about the famous explorer, included in the "Poetry Selections" chapter.

The Saint Lawrence (NF, 2) by William Toye: the history of Canada according to the great river. It describes the events and people in light of the importance the St. Lawrence had on the development of Canadian history. Many anecdotes and documents are quoted throughout the book, as well as good use of maps to fill in details.

*He Went With Champlain** (F, 2) by Louise Andrews Kent: The author chronicles the life, discoveries, and commitment of Samuel de Champlain. His life is observed through the eyes of a young and faithful servant who sees Champlain through to the end of his days. Particularly significant is Champlain's commitment to spread the Christian faith and the French culture in the New World. Attention to detail, and the chronology of failures and successes of his mission make this book an excellent addition to Canadian history study.

The First Canadian (F, 2, GSC) by C.T. Ritchie: Champlain's lifework was his desire to colonize Canada for his mother country of France. This story takes us from his first voyage to the New World through his many trials, until his death.

The Great Canoe (F, 1, BB) by Adelaide Leitch: A Huron father and his young son build a canoe as a gift to Champlain. The canoe proves to be a greater gift than any would realize.

The Man Who Was Always First (NF, 3) by Thomas Costain (Cavalcade of the North): A short story of Etienne Brule, the enterprising Frenchman who served Champlain, and in the end, committed treachery against him.

Henry Hudson, Captain of the Icebound Seas (F, 1) by Carl Carmer: Henry Hudson's trials of exploration, and the successes and failures he encountered are retold in this story. This early reader is optimistic about what may have happened to Hudson and his crew.

*Henry Hudson (NF, 2) by Ronald Syme: Henry Hudson fails repeatedly to find the elusive Northwest Passage. His merciful treatment toward his crew becomes his undoing, as the crew eventually mutinies against him because of their fear of exploring the cold northern seas. Although he never found the passage, his discovery and careful charting of the Hudson Bay earned him his mark in history. The Hudson Bay became the most significant trading route for Canadian goods going to Europe.

Mutiny On The Bay (F, 2, GSC) by R.S. Lambert: A compelling story of explorer Captain Henry Hudson and his mission to discover the Northwest Passage as taken from the daily journal of Habakuk Prickett, the virtuous and devout servant of the ship's owner.   Readers experience first hand the plight of those courageous and faith filled sailors as they battle the elements of the Arctic waters on the ship Discovery.   Hudson's stubbornness and refusal to turn back when all seems futile causes the crew's courage to turn to desperation, leading to a mutiny and the end of Captain Hudson and his allies.

Redcoat Sailor (F, 2, GSC) by R. S. Lambert: Sir Howard Douglas' adventurous life is spent serving in the British army in England, Canada and Spain. He then is appointed Lieutenant-Governor of New Brunswick.   The story portrays heroic virtue, courage and resourcefulness under trying circumstances and disaster.

***River of Canada**   (NF, 2) by Thomas Bredin: This book covers the scope and history of the St. Lawrence River. By looking at life in Europe, the author depicts what drove the early explorers, traders and missionaries to press on to greater trials, and how the river played its role.

The Rise and Fall of New France: (1610's-1760's)

There are several short stories listed in this section from a book of collected works called *Cavalcade of the North* edited by George Nelson. They are short stories of New France, all written by Thomas Costain, and listed as "Vignettes of French Canada." These vignettes are from Thomas Costain's history book on French Canada, *The White and The Gold*.

The First Settler (NF, 3) by Thomas Costain (Cavalcade of the North): A short story of Louis Hebert, the first man who settled in Canada. His steadfast spirit is evident from the legacy he left.

Maria Chapdelaine (NF, 3) by Louis Hemon: A classic story of faith, duty and romance set in New France. Life for the early French settlers is accurately depicted.

*Shadow on the Rock (NF, 3) by Willa Cather: The narrative of the life of Cecile, a girl who has come to Quebec from France with her father. Her father is the apothecary to Frontenac.

Frontenac (NF, 2) by Ronald Syme: Adventurous biography of the feisty Frontenac whose life work became establishing and defending the French colonies of Canada. This is an excellent history of the ongoing French-English rivalry, and the contest for support from the native population on both sides.

Frontenac and the Iroquois (F, 2, GSC) by Fred Swayze: Defending New France, building trust amongst the Native people, and establishing the strength of the settlements in New France were the legacy that Frontenac gave to Canada. His life and work are carefully drawn in this story.

The King's Loon (NF, 1) by Mary Alice Downie: Young Andre is a stowaway on an expedition of the new Count Frontenac to subdue the Iroquois and build Fort Frontenac. In this short novel, through the eyes of Andre we see a picture of the impact of Frontenac on New France.

Tonty (F, 2) by F. Swayze: Tonty and La Salle and their adventures in the Canadian wilderness spin a tale of intrigue and excitement. Tonty's impression of the missionary priests he encounters alters his belief of what is important in life.

Saint Isaac and the Indians (F, 2) by Milton Lomask: This book is a biography of Isaac Jogues, Jesuit missionary priest to New France in the 1640's. This is a beautiful story of evangelization in the New World and the martyrdom of brave missionaries.

Fire Over Huronia (F, 2-3) by Fred Swayze: Jean Amiot lives with the Jesuit Missionaries and with the Hurons in New France. This well written story provides insight into the native way of life, and portrays the heroic virtue lived out by the missionaries.

The Huron Carol (Christmas Carol) by St. Jean de Brebeuf: St. Jean de Brebeuf penned the first Canadian Christmas carol as a gift and teaching tool for the Huron people. It tells of the birth of Christ, the poverty into which he was born, and the gift of salvation. Included in the "Poetry Selections" chapter.

*Brebeuf and His Brethren (poem) by E. J. Pratt: This is an epic poem written in blank verse that retells in detail the life of the Canadian Martyrs from 1625-1649. The prose is lovely; the poem is available at the Canadian Saints web site listed under "Resources," and is also available in book form as collected works by E. J. Pratt.

Blessed Marie of New France (F, 2) by Mary Fabyan Windeatt: Mother Marie de L'Incarnacion comes from France with members of the Ursuline order. They were the first missionary sisters in Canada. An exceptional tale of faith and adventure.

Kateri Tekakwitha: Mohawk Maiden (NF, 2) by Evelyn Brown: Known as the Lily of the Mohawks, Kateri was a mystic, converted to Christianity by her acquaintance with the French missionaries. She was hated by her people and eventually suffered martyrdom for her faith.

*Mere Marie of the Ursulines (NF, 3) by Agnes Repplier: Mere Marie's young life prior to her entry into a convent and the historical and political situation of the times provide background for Mere Marie's adventures in New France. Some details of St. Ursula, whose charism is followed by Mere Marie, are included. Canadian history is woven beautifully and humorously into the story of Mere Marie's simple life in New France.

The King's Daughter (F, 3) by Suzanne Martel: An eighteen year old girl, orphaned as a child and brought up in a convent, comes to New France to marry as one of the "King's Girls." She is to marry a man whose first wife has died and who needs a mother for his children.

The Kings Girls (NF, 3) by Thomas Costain (Cavalcade of the North): A short account of the young women sent to the colony in New France as wives for the unmarried men settling the area.

Father Marquette and the Great River (F, 2) by August Derleth: This book documents the life and travels of Pere Marquette, a missionary priest who travelled with explorer Joliet from Canada to the Mississippi, exploring and evangelizing the native population along the way. This book is a simple and beautiful re-telling of his life's mission and his courage.

*Pere Marquette: Priest, Pioneer, Adventurer (NF, 3) by Agnes Repplier: The story of a 17th century priest who becomes one of the first Europeans to travel down the Mississippi. The author's delightful poetic style takes us on a journey through the history of Canada to set the stage for her story. She weaves the history of the Mississippi, the culture of the native people, and the activities of the Jesuits into her entertaining narrative.

*The Martyrs (poem) by Archibald Lampman: a poem about the Jesuit Missionaries who gave their lives for the faith. Included in the "Poetry Selections" chapter.

Madeleine Takes Command (F, 2) by Ethel Brill: an exciting account of Madeleine de Verchere, a 14 year old girl who maintains protection of her family's fort against Iroquois attacks. By her ingenuity and determination, she takes charge of a dangerous harassment.

The Maiden at Castle Dangerous (NF, 3) by Thomas Costain (Cavalcade of the North): A short tale of Madeleine de Verchere.

The Death of the Great Bishop (NF, 3) by Thomas Costain (Cavalcade of the North): A short vignette on the influence of Bishop Laval.

Fur Trade, Hudson Bay Company

Bay of the North – The Story of Pierre Radisson (F, 2) by Ronald Syme: Young Pierre Radisson's life is peppered with taking risks, suffering cruel consequences and experiencing incredible fortune. His bravery and sense of adventure keeps him moving and discovering all his life. His great desire to find the "Bay of the North" (Hudson Bay) keeps him wandering. The Ottawa River is too dangerous to continue to trade furs to Europe and he believes that the Bay will be the answer to prosperity for French Canada.

Runner of the Woods (NF, 2, GSC) by C.T. Ritchie: Pierre Radisson, an adventuresome fur trader and explorer spends much of his life living among the Mohawks. His knowledge of their ways, his wanderlust, and his desire to establish fur trade routes ultimately lead to his involvement in the developing Hudson's Bay Company. A clear picture is given of the relations between the Iroquois and the European traders.

With Pipe, Paddle and Song (F, 2) by Elizabeth Yates: An adventurous story of the rugged life of the Canadian voyageurs. A story that chronicles these men's daily lives as they travel the Canadian wilderness in search of furs for trading.   Faith, history and adventure come to life.

*The Voyageurs (poem) by John F. McDonnell: a poem about the Canadian voyageurs.   Included in the "Poetry Selections" chapter.

Fur Trader, the Story of Alexander Henry (F, 2) by Robert D. Ferguson: From the journals of Alexander Henry's travels throughout the Canadian wilderness, this story is brought to life. Henry is one of the earliest British fur traders, and owed his great success to his ability to relate to the native people and their ways.   A direct quote from his journal, "A series of events more like dreams than realities, more like fiction than truth."

Little Giant of the North by (F, 1-2) Alida Malkus: Henry Kelsey follows the example of his hero and mentor, Pierre Radisson, making trade successful for the Hudson's Bay Company.   Many of the British people cannot understand that friendship with and respect for the native people will increase the success of their trade but Henry quietly maintains good relations.

Fur Trader of the North (NF, 2) by Ronald Syme: Pierre de la Verendrye, a fur trader, with his four sons, did much to open up the route to Western Canada.   Their adventures led them to establish trading posts and a search for the "Western Sea," the Pacific Ocean.

Hudson's Bay Company (NF, 2) by Richard Morenus: The story of the Hudson's Bay Company beginning with Pierre Radisson and including his capture by the Iroquois as a boy to his explorations with Groseillier. Many other daring adventurers' stories are told including Kelsey and D'Iberville. This is an historical account of the rivalry between the Hudson's Bay Company and the Northwest Company up to the Metis Uprisings. These uprisings are observed from the point of view of the white settlers and the Canadian government, not the Metis perspective.

The Nor'Westers (NF, 2, GSC) by Marjorie Wilkins Campbell: This story outlines the rivalry between The Northwest Company and the Hudson's Bay Company over the fur trade in Canada. The two companies finally end their rivalry in a merge in 1820.

*The Last Fort (F, 2) by Elizabeth Coatsworth: Alexis, a young man coming of age, is sent in his father's footsteps as a voyageur, to secure land in the French territory of Illinois. His unlikely party travel the Mississippi from their home in Canada, which has been taken under British rule. Challenge and misfortune are dealt to Alexis, but ultimately a strong will and immovable morality help to accomplish the goal of proving his manhood by gaining a safe home for his family in French territory.

Forts of Canada (NF, 1-3) by A. M. Owens and Jane Yelland: An introduction to the forts built throughout Canadian history. Several hands on activities included. The perfect tool to use along with a field trip to an actual fort.

Adventure from the Bay (NF, 2, GSC) by Clifford Wilson: This story relays the lives of the men who made the Hudson's Bay Company, and ensured its future with their courage and dedication.

Fur and Gold (F, 2) by Roderick Haig-Brown: Outlining the settlement of British Columbia, the fur trade and the beginnings of government, this book provides an understanding of what was happening in Western Canada. Explores the impact the B.C. gold rush had on economics and settlement in the west, and on relationships with the native people.

Expulsion of the Acadians

A Proper Acadian (F, 1) by M.A. Downie and G. Rawlyk: One boy's experience of being sent away from Boston, his homeland, to live with the Acadians.

***Evangeline and the Acadians** (NF, 2) by Robert Tallant: The poem by Longfellow "Evangeline" is brought to life through this lovely historical narrative. Stanzas from "Evangeline" are used to show the emotional drama that the Acadians suffered.   Much background information is provided to the poem.

Evangeline (poem) by Henry Wadsworth Longfellow: The story of the tragedy of a young woman's life when the Acadians were removed from their home. (Available as an audio tape from St. Francis Books, see Resources Chapter.)

Evangeline for Children (F, 1-3, storybook) by Alice Couvillon and Elizabeth Moore: This simple re-telling of the Acadian expulsion is viewed through the eyes of the character of Longfellow's poem "Evangeline." Beautifully illustrated.

Escape from Grand Pre (F, 1, BB) by Frances C. Thompson: A family is torn apart by the exile of the Acadians by the British.   This easy-to-read novel depicts the exile, escape and eventual reunion of the Melanson family.

*A Land Divided (F, 2) by John F. Hayes: Families and lands are divided in this story of an Acadian woman married to a British officer and their son, who is caught trying to grasp the meaning of the conflict between the British and the French. An adventurous and sensitively written story depicting both sides of a heart wrenching event.

Seven Years War
(or, The French and Indian Wars) 1689-1763

Battle for the Rock: The Story of Wolfe and Montcalm (F, 2-3, GSC) by Joseph Schull: This book is an intense account of the events leading up to the battle of the Plains of Abraham, and of the battle itself.

*Drummer Boy for Montcalm (F, 2) by Wilma Pitchford Hays: Young Peter arrives in Quebec from France, and serves his mother country loyally. His devotion to his leader, Montcalm, the battle for Quebec, and Peter's sad acceptance of the French loss to the English weave together a fascinating tale, all based on a true story.

With Wolfe in Canada or The Winning of a Continent (F, 3) by G.A. Henty: James Walsham, an icon of heroic virtue, becomes involved in the struggle between England and France for the control of the North American continent. The author is renowned for his historical accuracy woven into a thrilling tale where the battle of Wolfe and Montcalm becomes a pivotal element in Canadian history.

Plains of Abraham (poem) by Charles Sangster: a poem about the battle of the Plains of Abraham.

Indian Captive (F, 2) by Lois Lenski: In 1758, during the French and Indian Wars, Mary Jemison is captured by Indian warriors and traded into slavery. She eventually becomes a daughter to her tribe and chooses to stay with them.

*Calico Captive** (F, 2) by Elizabeth George Speare: On the brink of war, a young family is forced from their home. Miriam, an adolescent American girl of British Puritan background, her sister and their family are captured by Indians and sold into slavery of French Canadians. Offers a subtle and interesting perspective to Canadian history, as Miriam's fears are assuaged and confirmed about the Native people and about the French. Her bias against Catholics is subdued as she observes the practice and worship of their faith.

Mohawk Valley (NF, 3, GSC) by Ronald Welch: A comfortable life at Cambridge is drastically altered for Alan Carey, who finds himself in the middle of the famous battle of Wolfe and Montcalm. He serves General Wolfe, drawing on his experience and courage to play a part in Britain's successful capture of Quebec. A powerful dramatization of the building antagonism between England and the French colonists.

Guns At Quebec (F, 2) by Allan Dwight: Steven Eliot from Colonial Boston is kidnapped by warring Indians, and sold into slavery of a French gentleman. His master is involved in the illicit activities of the Intendant. Steve is involved in the tense political affairs, and is also fond of the French families who are treated as badly as the English under the Intendant's iron fist and crooked affairs.

Father Gabriel's Cloak (F, 1, BB) by B.G. Swayze: A Young French settler, Marie, mistaken for a boy is carried away from her family in an Iroquois attack. After many years and a providential meeting with Father Gabriel, Tonty and La Salle, she is reunited with her family. Father Gabriel's loving presence, intercession and martyrdom become the reason and purpose for the miracles she experiences.

The Rover (NF, 2, GSC) by Thomas H. Raddall: During the Napoleonic wars, privateers (ships granted legal rights to pirate) guarded the coast of Canada and the US to prevent attacks and pirating from enemy ships. The Rover was a privateering vessel manned by Nova Scotians.

Immigration of United Empire Loyalists

*Johnny Tremain (F, 2) by Esther Forbes: This book is considered classic historical fiction of the American Revolution, the fight for independence from Britain. This would be a good choice to provide background information on Revolution, which led to the migration of the Loyalists.

Charlotte (F, storybook) by Janet Lunn: This is a true story of young Charlotte, a Canadian girl whose life is profoundly affected by the American Revolution. Her family is torn apart as a result of supporting two different sides of the war.

Drums of Niagara (F, 2) by Eric Acland: The fight for democracy, in the days of British Canada was a hard won battle by hand. This is a story of one man's struggle to build a nation out of the wilds.

Son of the Hawk (F, 3) by Thomas Raddall: Young David Strang of Nova Scotia is caught in the upheaval of the American Revolution. His family and community is torn apart by divided loyalties, to England and to the American colonies. He fights for Nova Scotia to become the "Fourteenth American colony," lives his life as both hero and traitor and comes to terms with the bitter disappointment of the American loss of Nova Scotia.

Escape. Adventure of a Loyalist Family and **Beginning Again, Further Adventures of a Loyalist Family** (F, 2) by Mary Beacock Fryer: These two books portray the escape of a loyalist family into Canada, and settling into their new life and new home from the point of view of their 12 year old son.

*On Loyalist Trails** (F, 2) by John F. Hayes: Davey Hunter is a young man whose loyalist family is transplanted out of the U.S. Life is hard for the British loyalists in the years following the American War of Independence. Davey's father leads a troubled escape into Canada. Their difficulties served to develop the new province of New Brunswick. His father's virtuous leadership strengthens a destitute people.

Raiders of the Mohawk: the Story of Butler's Rangers (NF, 2, GSC) by Orlo Miller: The Springer family, loyal to the British government, must find their way north to Canada to live in safety. They come under the protection of "Butler's Rangers," fighting the American rebels to maintain British control. The story of Walter Butler unfolds, and when defeat ultimately ends the war, the Springers, along with many other loyalists re-make their homes in Nova Scotia.

War of 1812

"Adventures in Canadian History, Battles of 1812"
by Pierre Berton
The Capture of Detroit
The Death of Isaac Brock
The Revenge of the Tribes
The Battle of Lake Erie
Canada Under Siege
The Death of Tecumseh

Jeremy's War 1812 (NF, 2) by John Ibbitson: A series of unfortunate events in Jeremy's life place him under the care of British soldiers. He becomes a personal servant of one of Canada's military heroes, General Isaac Brock, and is involved in saving Canada from American occupation.

Laura's Choice, the Story of Laura Secord (F, 2) by Connie Crook: This true story tells of Laura's childhood and of her daring journey to warn of the coming invasion of the American army.

The Good Soldier (NF, 2, GSC) by D.J. Goodspeed: Isaac Brock gives his life for Canada in battle against large American troops invading to occupy Canadian territory. His strategy and sacrifice ensures Canada's independence.

Brock (poem) by Charles Sangster: A poem about the life of one of the heroes of the War of 1812. Included in the "Poetry Selections" chapter.

Treason at York (F, 2-3) by John Hayes: Dramatic historical fiction, using accurate information as a backdrop for a story of the War of 1812 in the city of York (now Toronto).

***Tecumseh** (F, 2, GSC) by Luella Bruce Creighton: In this beautifully written tale of the life of Tecumseh, the Shawnee chief, we meet a great orator who gave his life to unite the native tribes scattered across North America. He defied both American fighting tactics and the native practice of torture to become a hero in his own day and a legend of courage and compassion.

The Rowboat War (NF, 2, GSC) by Fred Swayze: The battles of the War of 1812 included a battle of Canadians in rowboats, who came to aid the British, against armed American warships, under the leadership of Robert Livingston.

The Scout Who Led an Army (F, 1, BB) by Lareine Ballantyne: Based on the true story of Billy Green, this book describes a decisive battle of the War of 1812. Nineteen year old Billy leads British and Canadian troops to an American camp for a sneak attack.

Adventure at the Mill (F, 1, BB) by Barbara and Heather Bramwell: A family finds a young black boy hiding at their home during the War of 1812. A picture of life during the war for young readers.

Underground Railway (1830's – 1860's)

*Across Five Aprils (F, 3) by Irene Hunt: A beautiful story of a family's struggles during the American Civil War. Excellent insight is given to the nature of slavery, of humanity, and of the battle, internal and external, personal and societal against evil. Through Tom, a young boy coming of age during this period in history, the reader gains an understanding of both the events and emotions of the Civil War. A good choice to start a study on the slave migration to freedom in Canada.

The Red Badge of Courage (F, 3) by Stephen Crane: Set in the US, scenes from the battlefield of the Civil War portrayed by a young soldier. An excellent choice for highschoolers to understand the intensity of the fight for freedom from slavery.

The Drinking Gourd (F, 1) by F.N. Monjo: A young boy helps a family of escaped slaves follow the "Big Dipper" or drinking gourd to freedom in Canada.

The Last Safe House (F and NF, 1-3) by Barbara Greenwood: A black family escapes slavery by fleeing north to Canada. The fictional family's tale is interwoven with sidebars of historical information, details about the way of life for fugitive slaves and for those people helping them to freedom.   Highlights some of the courageous people who fought for freedom.

Brady (F, 2) by Jean Fritz: Brady is caught in a secret of the Underground Railway that he is uncertain he can keep. His father, a minister in a small town, is shunned by townspeople, friends and congregation when he speaks out against slavery.   This story is set in the US, but is a suspenseful account of the people who helped runaway slaves escape to Canada.

*****Underground to Canada** (F, 2) by Barbara Smucker: Two young slave girls from the southern US escape for a chance of freedom in Canada. An accurate picture of the "underground railroad," how people aided escaped slaves, and the trials they endured.

Rebellion of 1837

Rebels Ride at Night (F, 2) by John Hayes: With authority, accuracy and adventure the author relays the tale of the Rebellion of 1837 led by William Lyon Mackenzie King.

The Boy with an R in His Hand (F, 1-2) by James Reaney: Captivating tale about two orphaned boys in York (now Toronto) who inadvertently get caught up in the politics of the day. William Lyon Mackenzie King battles the Tories through his newspaper, and the boys help him take up the battle cry of "freedom of the press!"

*A Question of Loyalty (F, 2) by Barbara Greenwood: Deborah discovers and hides a young rebel. She struggles with the conflict of deceiving her family and the danger of harbouring an "enemy."

Rebel on the Trail (F, 2) by Lynn Cook: Two children become involved in the political drama of the day. The author reveals the thoughts of the children as they experience first hand the impact of the uprising.

Western Exploration

*Alexander Mackenzie, Canadian Explorer (NF, 2) by Ronald Syme: Mackenzie's trials, adventures and fortitude are brought to life by the author's attention to detail and historical accuracy.

A Dog Came Too (NF, story book) by Ainslie Manson and Ann Blades: The true story of "our dog," the dog that went with Alexander Mackenzie's exploration to the Pacific Ocean. He was the first dog to make the long journey west by land.

From Sea to Sea (F, 3) by Thomas Bredin: The trials of Alexander Mackenzie and his valiant crossing of an enormous country, to reach the Pacific coast by a land route. Quotes from the explorer's account of his journey are used to provide insight and realism to the story.

Captain of the Discovery (F, 2, GSC) by Roderick Haig-Brown: the voyages of Captain George Vancouver when he sailed with Cook, and on his own to continue Cook's work of charting the coast of the Pacific Northwest.

*The Farthest Shores (F, 2-3) by Roderick Haig-Brown: fascinating tales of the men who deigned to chart the western shores of Canada, the British Columbia coastline, by sea and by land. Bering, Cook, Vancouver, Mackenzie, Fraser and Thompson.

Fur and Gold (F, 2) by Roderick Haig-Brown: Outlining the settlement of British Columbia, the fur trade and the beginnings of government, this book provides an understanding of what was happening in western Canada. It explores the impact the B.C. gold rush had on economics and settlement in the west, and on relationships with the native people.

The Map-Maker (F, 2, GSC) by Kerry Wood: Chronicle of the life of David Thompson, whose great accomplishment was the mapping of western Canada.

The Savage River: Seventy-one Days With Simon Fraser (F, 2, GSC) by M. Wilkins Campbell: From the journals of Simon, the story of the first team of white men to journey down the Fraser River and back. A story of courageous leadership, hope and disappointment.

Vancouver, Explorer of the Pacific Coast (F, 1) by Ronald Syme: Captain George Vancouver's adventures exploring the west coast of North America.

Opening the West, RCMP and Railways

"Adventures in Canadian History, Canada Moves West" by Pierre Berton

A Prairie Nightmare
The Men in Sheepskin Coats
Steel Across the Plains
The Railway Pathfinders

Kids Book of Railways (NF, 2) by Pat Hancock: A beautifully illustrated book telling the history of Canada's railway. Like other "Kids Books" by Kids Can Press, this is excellent for all ages as there is so much visual content.

*The Bold Heart (F, 2, GSC) by Josephine Phelan: The story of Father Lacombe, a missionary to the Canadian North West. He acted as a peacemaker between the builders of the transcontinental railway and the natives who did not want their land invaded. He lived with the native people, sharing their ways and sharing the Gospel. Westward expansion is seen vividly in this book.

Buckskin Colonist (F, 2) by John Hayes: The Selkirk settlers who came to the Red River in 1812 to farm are now in a bitter conflict with the fur traders, who do not want settlers in "fur country".

Driven from their homes in Scotland, the sturdy settlers fight hard and long for the right to farm the Red River Valley.

*Bugles in the Hills** (F, 2) by John Hayes: The North West Mounted Police came into existence as a result of the illicit trafficking of alcohol to the Native population. Their culture and trade were being devastated by this treatment; the Canadian government responds to this by providing law enforcement for the West. Young Bill Walton's ambition is to join the newly formed NWMP.

The Queen's Cowboy (F, 2, GSC) by Kerry Wood: This is the biography of James Mcleod and story of the beginnings of the NWMP. Other historical events tie into the remarkable life of MacLeod; the Riel Rebellion, Custer's last stand, the opening of rail across the West, and the development of the western cities and provinces.

The Scarlet Force and **The Force Carries On** (NF, 2, GSC) by T. Morris Longstreth: The first twenty years of the Mounted Police were spent taming the Canadian West in the Scarlet Force. The Force Carries On tells the story of the refinement and scope of the Mounties activities until modern times.

The Steel Ribbon (F, 2) by John F. Hayes: The section of railway around the cliffs of Lake

Superior was some of the most dangerous and difficult rail to be laid in North America. This tale of high adventure depicts the courage and determination of men who battled the wilderness to overcome it.

Coolies (F, storybook) by Yin: Two young Chinese brothers come to America to work on the railway. The loving relationship between the two brothers is exemplified as they suffer due to the unjust treatment of the Chinese workers.   This book discusses traditional Chinese beliefs. Beautifully illustrated.

Settling of the West

The Great Chief (NF, 2, GSC) by Kerry Wood: Maskapatoon is greatly respected amongst two great Indian Nations, the Cree and the Blackfoot, for his courage, power and success in war. Despite his success as a warrior, he seeks to find meaning of a vision that he is given. He learns to value peace, and ultimately a Methodist pastor leads him to conversion. Because of the respect he has earned, he is able to travel amongst the tribes, promoting his new mission of peace.

Red River Adventure (NF, 2, GSC) by J. W. Chalmers: Lord Selkirk of Scotland buys huge tracts of land from the Hudson Bay Company to settle dispossessed farmers of Ireland and Scotland in Canada. He and his appointed Governor are up against the fur traders who do not want their trade affected by the settlers.

Petranella (F, storybook) by Betty Waterton: Petranella is a young girl whose family is leaving to homestead in Canada. She experiences joy and sadness as she leaves her home and her family establishes a new life.

1866 Fenian Uprising

The Ballad of D'Arcy McGee (NF, 2, GSC) by Josephine Phelan: see entry under "Life in the 1800's."

Spy in the Shadows F, 2) by Barbara Greenwood: Set in the time of pending Confederation, a threat of Irish immigrants uprising against the British, this story accurately portrays the danger that lurks in the hearts of the Fenians.   Liam is confused about where his support should be and his maturity is clear in the character development of this novel.

Riel (or Northwest) Rebellion

Storm at Batoche (F, 1, storybook) by Maxine Trottier: The fictional story of a young boy who meets Louis Riel and experiences the conflict between Canada's Catholic Metis (mixed French and Native heritage) and the English speaking Protestant communities first hand.

My Uncle Joe (F, 2) by James Mcnamee: A young boy is to be cared for by his uncle, who has a great love for Louis Riel. Throughout the story, Riel comes into the story only peripherally, but the reader gains an understanding, through a sarcastic humour, of the tension between the Metis and the English who wanted their land.

Revolt in the West (NF, 2, GSC) by Edward McCourt: This is the story of the life of Louis Riel, and the circumstances that led to the Riel Rebellion.

Flaming Prairies (F, 2-3) by John F. Hayes: A splendid re-telling of the adventures of the Rebellion of 1885. Another captivating novel by Mr. Hayes based on accurate historical detail.

A Very Small Rebellion (F, 2) by Jan Truss: Two stories are interwoven here; the story of Louis Riel and the Metis Rebellions is juxtaposed with a modern racial land conflict. Three grade 7 Metis/ Native students living in a settlement are faced with the expropriation of their land to make way for a new road.

Buckskin Brigadier (NF, 2, GSC) by Edward McCourt: In 1885, the Alberta Field force, a group of Canadian militia, under the leadership of Tom Strange, is formed to prevent the Cree uprising of the Northwest Rebellion.

Northwest Passage/ Arctic Exploration

"Adventures in Canadian History, Exploring the Frozen North" by Pierre Berton
Dr. Kane of the Arctic Seas
Jane Franklin's Obsession
Parry of the Arctic
Trapped in the Arctic

On Foot in the Arctic (NF, 2) by Ronald Syme: Samuel Hearne's exploration of the "Barren Lands" west of the Hudson Bay was the first exploration of the Canadian north by a European. This story traces his travels with the Hudson's Bay Company.

The Link Between the Oceans (NF, 2-3) by Leslie Neatby: The history of the search for the Northwest Passage gathered primarily through the journals of a young missionary. John Miertsching was invited on the voyages in search of the ill-fated Franklin expedition because he had lived amongst the people of the North as a missionary, and he was familiar with their ways and spoke their language. A fascinating perspective of exploration.

The True North (NF, 2, GSC) by T.C Fairley and Charles Israel: Captain Joseph Bernier and his passion for ships and arctic exploration led to the claiming of the arctic islands for Canada.   This is the story of his life and accomplishments.

British Columbia Gold Rush

Quest in the Cariboo (F, 2) by John Hayes: This is a suspenseful and well told tale of a boy setting out to find his brother, after he hears that his brother has met disaster during his search for gold in the Cariboo.

West to the Cariboo (F, 1, BB) by Lorrie McLauglin: Two brothers head west to find their father, who left three years before on a rumour of gold in British Columbia.

Moses, Me and Murder (F, 1-2) by Ann Walsh: Set during the B.C. Gold Rush, a boy gets pulled into the scene of a murder mystery.

The Man with the Yellow Eyes (F, 1, BB) by Catherine Anthony Clark: Two young boys discover a scoundrel who plans to cheat their father out of his stake on a mine. They devise a plan to ensure the claim.

*Fur and Gold by Roderick Haig-Brown: (see listing under Western Exploration)

Klondike Gold Rush

"Adventures in Canadian History, The Klondike Stampede" by Pierre Berton

Before the Gold Rush

Bonanza Gold
City of Gold
Kings of the Klondike
The Klondike Stampede
Trails of '98

Gold Rush Fever: A Story of the Klondike (F, NF, 2)
by Barbara Greenwood: Another excellent Barbara Greenwood book, a fictional tale of two boys adventure of the Klondike Gold Rush. Interwoven with activities and sidebars of historical and geographical information.

The Cremation of Sam McGee (poem) by Robert Service: There is a beautifully illustrated version of this poem, and "The Shooting of Dan McGrew," by Canadian artist Ted Harrison. As well as exceptional paintings depicting the awesome Canadian north, there is an excellent commentary for each picture and stanza of these poems (this version is published by Kids Can Press).

*__The Golden Trail__ (NF, 2, GSC) by Pierre
Berton: The full story of the moil and madness of
the Klondike Gold Rush, how it began, and what
brought about its abrupt end.   Fascinating,
incredible, and tragic.   A fine example of reality
being more bizarre than fiction.

Pioneers/ Life in the 1800's

The Dangerous Cove (F, 2) by John F. Hayes: A high adventure story set on the coast of Newfoundland. A tale of piracy and early settlers.

The Ballad of D'Arcy McGee (NF, 2, GSC) by Josephine Phelan: This story chronicles the colourful life of the charismatic D'Arcy McGee, one of the fathers of Confederation. His dramatic story and tragic end make a stirring political tale.

A Pioneer Story: The Daily Life of a Canadian Family in 1840 (F and NF, 2) by Barbara Greenwood: A young family pioneering in the early days of Canada.

A Pioneer Thanksgiving by Barbara Greenwood: A supplement to A Pioneer Story detailing a special event in the lives of a pioneering family.

Pioneer Crafts by Barbara Greenwood: A supplementary craft and activity book to go along with A Pioneer Story.

The New Land: A First Year on the Prairie: (F, 1, storybook) by Marilynn Reynolds: A family leaves their homeland of England, to carve out a life in the Canadian Prairie. A lovely Canadian companion to the "Little House" series.

Danger in the Coves (F, 1, BB) by Frances C. Thompson: The Cameron family has many adventures living in Old Quebec in the 1800's; families everywhere are faced with their sons being kidnapped by crimps to work on trade vessels. A fire that destroys much of Quebec is seen through the eyes of young Davy Cameron.

Pioneer Girl (NF, 2) by Maryanne Caswell: A series of letters are compiled to create a beautiful picture of pioneer life. These actual letters are written by young Maryanne Caswell to her grandmother about her family's adventures travelling from their home in Ontario to Saskatoon.

The Backwoods of Canada (NF, 3) by Catherine Parr Traill: Published originally in 1836, a woman describes, through a series of detailed letters, the domestic life in the "backwoods," when she comes from England to join her husband.

The Adventures of Billy Topsail (F, 2) by Norman Duncan: The grand tale of the life of a boy and his brave dog on the coast of Newfoundland.

The Last Voyage of the Scotian, First Spring on Grand Banks, The Shantymen at Cache Lake, Trouble at Lachine Mill (F and NF, 2) series by Bill Freeman: This series of four books all revolve around the life and adventures of a brother and sister, John and Meg Bains. The stories take place in the late 1800's, and the author includes many actual photographs of the areas and events he is describing, as well as a glossary of terms. An accurate and vivid picture of Canadian life in the 1800's is provided.

*They Sought a New Land (NF, storybook, 1-3) by William Kurelek: A beautiful overview of the lives of immigrants to Canada and the U.S. Told through quotes, narrative and paintings, the difficult life of the immigrant is revealed. Why they left Europe, how they came to the New World, how they lived, celebrated their faith and traditions, and how they kept in touch with and blended their many heritages in a new land are depicted in this book.

Anne of Green Gables series (F, 2) by L.M. Montgomery: Life on Prince Edward Island in the late 1800's is experienced through the eyes of the irrepressible Anne, her childhood, education, marriage and motherhood in this series of delightful books. Anne comes to a family as an unwanted orphan, and captures the hearts of the Cuthbert family and all who meet her.

The Salt-Water Men (NF, 2, GSC) by Joseph Schull: This is the story of Canada's deep sea sailors, their work and the changes that came about for sailors, ships and trade in the nineteenth century.

Lukey-Paul from Labrador (F, 1, BB) by Adelaide Leitch: Lukey-Paul is a young trapper, who is cheated out of an extraordinary find in his trap. His resolve takes him along the Labrador coast in a steamer as a stowaway.

The Heroine of Long Point (F, 1, BB) by Leslie and Lois Benham: Based on a true story, this is the adventure of a daring woman who rescued the crew of a ship run aground.

Turn of the Century, World War I and its Aftermath (1900-1920's)

Anne of Green Gables series (F, 2) by L.M. Montgomery: see review in "Life in the 1800's" section.

Days of Terror (F, 2) by Barbara Smucker: This expressively written book tells the story of Peter Neufeld, a Mennonite boy. Beginning in a peaceful village in Russia, it describes the ominous warnings of revolution and the days filled with starvation, fear and poverty. These threats are realized. The Mennonites decide that they must emigrate as their religion is threatened, and at last they find new hope when they arrive in Canada.

The Halifax Disaster (NF, 2) by Ernest Fraser Robinson: The author provides an account of the disaster that takes place in Halifax in 1917, when a freighter carrying explosives collides with another ship. He writes as someone witnessing the events as they happen. The book includes photos and eye witness accounts.

Knights of the Air (NF, 2, GSC) by John Norman Harris: Canada's impact on military history is seen through the feats of the fighter pilots of Canada's air force during WWI.

Rilla of Ingleside (F, 2) by L.M. Montgomery:
Rilla is the daughter of Anne of Green Gables and
Gilbert Blythe. She experiences adolescence and
coming of age during the years of WWI.

Goodbye Sarah (F, 1) by Geoffrey Bilson:
Differing political views during the Winnipeg
General Strike in 1919 create tension in the
friendship of two young girls from different
families.

*In Flanders Fields (NF, 1-3) by Linda Granfield:
The story of the famous poem "In Flanders Fields"
penned by a young Canadian doctor fighting
overseas. Excellent background information on the
setting of the poem and WWI is included. This is a
good book to include in Canadian history studies
of WWI, and also to read each Remembrance Day.

Belle's Journey (F, storybook) by Marilynn
Reynolds: A young girl's faithful pony carries her
through a prairie snowstorm.

His Banner over Me (F, 2) by Jean Little: A young
girl's life in Canada with relatives while her parents
are away working as missionaries depicts her
personal growth and her war effort during WWI.
This story is based on the author's mother's
experiences.

Depression/World War II 1927-1945

Prairie Boy's Winter and *Prairie Boy's Summer* (NF, 1-3) by William Kurelek: These two books depict, through Kurelek's paintings and narrative, the Great Depression of his childhood. The simple day-to-day activities of farming, school days, games and family life are vividly told through his art and stories.

Pa's Harvest (F, 1, storybook) by Jan Andrews: Ephie's father, Pa, is a farmer who struggles and is nearly defeated by the Great Depression of the 1930's. Based on a true story, the author imparts a sense of how hardship strengthens people, and what matters most is the love that binds people.

*The Mitchells: Five for Victory, Canadian Summer, Friendly Gables (F, 2) by Hilda van Stockum: The Mitchell family experiences their father going off to war (WWII), and the aftermath of war time. The funny and touching moments of family life in times of trials, are beautifully portrayed by the author in this trilogy.

Trapp Family Singers (NF, 2-3) by Maria Augusta Trapp: The story that inspired the movie "The Sound of Music" is much more a story of faith than is portrayed in the movie. Part two of the book is the family's relocating to the US, after fleeing their homeland during the war. Their love of God and their charity is a testimony of their faith.

Ships of the Great Days (NF, 2, GSC) by Joseph Schull: This is the story of the development of Canada's Navy during the Second World War. Fighting steadily increasing technology, the Canadian ships and seamen patrolled the seas against the onslaught of the war.

Arctic Assignment (NF, 2, GSC) by Sgt. F.S. Farrar, RCMP: The St. Roch (a small wooden vessel) is sent on an RCMP assignment to patrol the Arctic islands and territory. The adventuresome voyage, begun in 1940, is retold by the author, who sailed on this assignment.

There are a few books that are set in Europe in WWI and WWII that are worth mentioning here, as they would be noteworthy complements to studying the Great Wars.

1917: Red Banners, White Mantle (NF, 3) by Dr. Warren H. Carroll: A fascinating history of the year 1917, in the midst of WWI. Includes Lenin, Rasputin, the saintly Emperor Charles, with Our Lady's apparitions at Fatima portrayed as the central event to which the dramatic events in other parts of the world are related. High school level; some characters, for example Rasputin, are shockingly evil. Dr. Carroll is a professor of history and founder of Christendom College.

The Good Master and ***The Singing Tree*** (F, 2) by Kate Seredy: The Good Master takes place before WWI in Hungary. It describes the life of a young girl who goes to live with her cousin, because her father cannot control her. In a wholesome family she blossoms. The Singing Tree is a sequel to The Good Master. Much more serious in tone, the family must meet the hardships of the war without the men, who have been drafted. Throughout their trials, there is great hope.

The Borrowed House (F, 2-3) by Hilda Van Stockum: A young German girl's education has been filled with propaganda. Through her curiosity, and a series of events, she comes to realize Nazi objectives.

Enemy Brothers: A Story of World War II (F, 2) by Constance Savery: An adventurous story set in England in the early years of WWII. A young British airman, Dym Ingleford, discovers that a Nazi boy, Max, who has fallen into British hands is really his younger brother who was kidnapped as a baby and raised in Germany. Dym brings the boy home to live with his large, happy family, but Max refuses to acknowledge them. The patient and loving kindness of the family gradually win Max over. He is then given the chance to return home to Germany. This book gives a nice impression of the English character. Good character development.

The Winged Watchman (F, 2) by Hilda Van Stockum: During the Nazi occupation of Holland, a family experiences hardship and sorrow. A sensitive story of courage, hope and faith. The author is descriptive of life during the war without being graphic.

The Sinking of the Bismarck (NF, 2) by William Shirer: This is the stirring story of the chase to sink the German battleship "Bismarck" by the British Navy during WWII.

The Shadow of His Wings (NF, 3) by Fr. Gereon Goldmann: This is a true account of a young German seminarian who is drafted into Hitler's army, against his will and his ideals. Finally ordained, he secretly ministers to soldiers and victims of the war.

Spaces provided after each heading of books in this list are intended for additions and notes that parents may want to include.

Chapter five: Timelines

Using and creating a timeline has become an important part of the process for studying history in our family. Besides providing a visual reference point, a timeline gives us an opportunity to research, to write and to share information with others. Not only people and events comprise a timeline, but inventions, ideas, world history or family history, anything that was discussed, or was of particular interest to your children can go on the timeline. It then becomes personal to your family about the main aspects of history, and also the things that were fun, interesting or meaningful to you. Our timelines are big, so they can include artwork and writing projects.

Ideally a timeline can be put up on a wall. Depending on the size of historical period you are studying, a timeline may take up quite a large space. A timeline to study the age of exploration could probably fit onto one piece of poster board, but a study involving the scope of Canadian history should be much larger. If wall space is a problem, the timeline can go into a book. I'll discuss some ideas for timelines first, then some ideas for making them in books. Heavy paper or poster board is best for a timeline, because it is sturdy. We usually cut poster board in half lengthwise and join the pieces end to end horizontally to whatever length we need. I like to use a nice bold colour so that any writing or pictures that we have used stand out.

Divide the timeline into equal "century" sections, and mark the century years clearly along the top or bottom of the timeline. All other information can be added in by putting it onto another piece of paper, cutting it out and taping or gluing it (use rubber cement so it doesn't bubble the paper) onto the poster board. We sometimes draw our own pictures of people or events, print them from the computer, or photocopy them from books we have used.

When children are writing, drawing or researching for a visual tool that shares information with other people, they are more likely to be motivated to write, which includes research and understanding of their topic. If they are allowed to choose topics that they are interested in, writing will be more joyful. Shorter writing projects can be put on the timeline in the appropriate centuries.

If wall space is impractical for a large timeline, a large, sturdy archive quality scrapbook is a good choice. It's worth the small amount more to purchase, as it will last for years, and pages can be purchased and added in as necessary. These scrapbooks are available at most craft stores and photography supply stores. We use the front inside page as a title page, and then every two pages that open out together as a century page. The top inch or two can be used to put in the years (every ten, twenty or fifty years for each century page, depending on how detailed the timeline is), and underneath that "timeline facts" there will still be a large space available where additional information can go, drawings or sketches suitable for that era, articles written by the children, or even information or pictures that are particularly fascinating can be added by photocopying or scanning them in.

Either way, if your timeline goes on the wall or in a book, it is a great way to review information and share it with others. At the end of a study, our family always puts our timelines into a book format; these "study books" are poured over many times.

Chapter six: Poetry and Art

POETRY

There is much Canadian poetry that has been written through our history. Poetry is important not only for memory work, but also because it reflects some of the thoughts, feelings and experiences of the people of our past. A sampling of poems in their entirety has been included here, subjectively chosen by the author. Most were chosen because they specifically represented a particular aspect of Canadian history, and all were chosen because they were in the public domain.

Also included is a list of some significant poets and titles of their poems. Where reasonable to do, in the chronological list of books, I've provided a cross reference so that parents can choose poetry to read alongside a novel.

There are hundreds of poets and poems available through a remarkably good resource that is a federal government website "National Archive of Poetry" (see resources chapter). Canadian poetry, like other areas of the arts in Canada, often reflects the theme of the contrast of beauty and harshness of the north. Early literary works struggle to find the Canadian "voice", a sense of identity that is difficult to attain, being such close neighbours with, and having so much in common with the United States. Early Canadian writers often sought to define what is essentially Canadian and to capture that in their works. Distinctly Canadian poetry emerges in the early 1800's. There are two significant aspects to our poetry, as we are a country with two official languages, and essentially two cultures. English speaking poets are included; there are links to French Canadian poets and their poetry listed on the National Archive of Poetry site.

JACQUES CARTIER
McGee, Thomas D'Arcy (1825-1868)

In the sea-port of Saint Malo
'twas a smiling morn in May,
When the Commodore Jacques Cartier
to the westward sailed away;
In the crowded old Cathedral
all the town were on their knees
For the safe return of kinsmen from the
undiscovered seas;
And every autumn blast that swept
o'er pinnacle and pier
Filled manly heart with sorrow,
and gentle hearts with fear.

A year passed o'er Saint Malo —
again came round the day
When the Commodore Jacques Cartier
to the westward sailed away;
But no tidings from the absent
had come the way they went,
And tearful were the vigils
that many a maiden spent;
And manly hearts were filled with gloom,
and gentle hearts with with fear.
When no tidings came from Cartier
at the closing of the they year.

But the earth is as the Future,
it hath its hidden side,
And the Captain of Saint Malo
was rejoicing in his pride
In the forests of the North —
while his townsmen mourned his loss.
He was rearing on Mount-Royal
the *fleur-de-lis* and cross;
And when two months were over
and added to the year,
Saint Malo hailed him home again,
cheer answering to cheer.

He told them of a region, hard,
iron-bound and cold,
Nor seas of pearl abounded,
nor mines of shining gold,
Where the wind from Thulè freezes
the word upon the lip,
And the ice in spring comes sailing
athwart the early ship;
He told them of the frozen scene
until they thrill'd with fear,
And piled fresh fuel on the hearth
to make them better cheer.

But when he chang'd the strain —
he told how soon is cast
In early Spring the fetters
that hold the waters fast;
How the Winter causeway broken
is drifted out to sea,
And the rills and rivers sing with pride
the anthem of the free;
How the magic wand of Summer
clad the landscape to his eyes,
Like the dry bones of the just,
when they wake in Paradise.

He told them of the Algonquin braves —
the hunters of the wild,
Of how the Indian mother
in the forest rocks her child;
Of how, poor souls, they fancy
in every living thing
A spirit good or evil,
that claims their worshipping;
Of how they brought their sick and maim'd
for him to breathe upon,
And of the wonders wrought for them
thro' the Gospel of St. John.

He told them of the river,
whose mighty current gave
Its freshness for a hundred leagues
to ocean's briny wave;
He told them of the glorious scene
presented to his sight,
What time he reared the cross and crown
on Hochelaga's height,
And of the fortress cliff that keeps
of Canada the key,
And they welcomed back Jacques Cartier
from this perils over sea.

THE MAPLE

Darnell, H. F., Rev., M.A.

All hail to the broad-leaved Maple!
  With its fair and changeful dress--
A type of our youthful country
  In its pride and loveliness;
Whether in Spring or Summer,
  Or in the dreary Fall,
'Mid Nature's forest children,
  She's fairest of them all.

Down sunny slopes and valleys
  Her graceful form is seen,
Her wide, umbrageous branches
  The sun-burnt reaper screen;
'Mid the dark-browed firs and cedars
  Her livelier colours shine,
Like the dawn of a brighter future
  On the settler's hut of pine.

She crowns the pleasant hill top,
  Whispers on breezy downs,
And casts refreshing shadows
  O'er the streets of our busy towns;
She gladdens the aching eye-ball,
  Shelters the weary head,
And scatters her crimson glories
  On the graves of the silent dead.

When Winter's frosts are yielding
  To the sun's returning sway,
And merry groups are speeding
  To sugar-woods away,
The sweet and welling juices,
  Which form their welcome spoil,
Tell of the teeming plenty
  Which here waits honest toil.

When sweet-voiced Spring, soft-breathing,
  Breaks Nature's icy sleep,
And the forest boughs are swaying
  Like the green waves of the deep;
In her fair and budding beauty,
  A fitting emblem she
Of this our land of promise,
  Of hope, of liberty.

And when her leaves, all crimson,
  Droop silently and fall,
Like drops of life-blood welling
  From a warrior brave and tall,
They tell how fast and freely
  Would her children's blood be shed,
Ere the soil of our faith and freedom
  Should echo a foeman's tread.

The hail to the broad-leaved Maple
  With her fair and changeful dress--
A type of our youthful country
  In its pride and loveliness;
Whether in Spring or Summer,
  Or in the dreary Fall,
'Mid Nature's forest children:
  She's fairest of them all.

THE VOYAGEUR'S SONG

M'Donnell, John F.

We track the herds o'er the prairies wide,
  Through the length of the summer day;
And guide the canoe on the rapid's tide,
  Where the waters flash in the ray;
Where the silvery scales of the salmon glance
  On the bosom of the pool:--
And we rest our wearied limbs at eve,
  In the shade of the pine-trees cool.
Let others toil for golden store;
  For riches little we care:
      Oh, the happiest life
      In this world of strife,
  Is that of a Voyageur.

When the red sun sinks in the golden West,
  At evening when he goes
With ministering hosts of the golden clouds,
  To seek the night's repose--
We pitch our tents on the soft green sward,--
  And we light our evening fire,--
And we mingle strains of our Northern land
  With the notes of the forest choir.
Time flies along, with jest and song,
  For our merry men are there:
      Oh there's not a life,
      In this world of strife,
  Like that of a Voyageur.

O sweet and soft our couches made,
  With the broad green summer leaves,
And the curtains spread above the head
  Are those which Nature weaves.
The tall oak and the spreading elm
  Are twined in a tangled screen,--
Surpassing far all the magic skill
  Of the sculptor's art e'er seen.
We shun the noise of the busy world,
  For there's crime and misery there;
    And the happiest life,
      In this world of strife,
  Is that of a Voyageur.

THE MARTYRS

Lampman, Archibald (1861-1899)

O ye, who found in men's brief ways no sign
  Of strength or help, so cast them forth, and threw
  Your whole souls up to one ye deemed most true,
Nor failed nor doubted but held fast your line,
Seeing before you that divine face shine;
  Shall we not mourn, when yours are now so few,
  Those sterner days, when all men yearned to you,
White souls whose beauty made their world divine:
Yet still across life's tangled storms we see,
  Following the cross, your pale procession led,
  One hope, one end, all others sacrificed,
Self-abnegation, love, humility,
  Your faces shining toward the bended head,
    The wounded hands and patient feet of Christ.

THE PLAINS OF ABRAHAM

Sangster, Charles

I stood upon the Plain,
That had trembled when the slain
Hurled their proud, defiant curses at the
battle-heated foe,
When the steed dashed right and left,
Through the bloody gaps he cleft,
When the bridle-rein was broken,
and the rider was laid low.

What busy feet had trod
Upon the very sod
Where I marshalled the battalions
of my fancy to my aid!
And I saw the combat dire,
Heard the quick, incessant fire,
And the cannon's echoes startling
the reverberating glade.

I heard the chorus dire,
That jarred along the lyre
On which the hymn of battle rung,
like surgings of the wave.
When the storm at blackest night,
Wakes the ocean in affright,
As it shouts its mighty pibroch o'er
some shipwrecked vessel's grave.

I saw the broad claymore
    Flash from its scabbard, o'er
The ranks that quailed and shuddered
at the close and fierce attack;
    When Victory gave the word,
    Auld Scotia drew the sword,
And with arm that never faltered
drove the brave defender back.

I saw two great chiefs die,
    Their last breaths like the sigh
Of the zephyr-sprite that wantons
on the rosy lips of morn;
    No envy-poisoned darts,
    No rancour in their hearts,
To unfit them for their triumph
over death's impending scorn.

And as I thought and gazed,
    My soul, exultant, praised
The Power to whom each mighty act
and victory are due,
    For the saint-like Peace that smiled
    Like a heaven-gifted child,
And for the air of quietude
that steeped the distant view.

Oh, rare, divinest life
Of peace, compared with Strife!
Yours is the truest splendor,
and the most enduring fame;
All the glory ever reaped
Where the fiends of battle leaped,
Is harsh discord to the music
of your undertoned acclaim.

SONG FOR CANADA

Sangster, Charles

Song of the race whose sires
Aroused the martial flame,
   That filled with smiles
   The triune Isles,
Through all their heights of fame!
With hearts as brave as theirs,
With hopes as strong and high,
   We'll ne'er disgrace
   The honored race
Whose deeds can never die.
  Let but the rash intruder dare
   To touch our darling strand,
    That martial fires
    That thrilled our sires
   Would flame throughout the land.

Our lakes are deep and wide,
Our fields and forests broad;
   With cheerful air
   We'll speed the share,
And break the fruitful sod;
Till blest with rural peace,
Proud of our rustic toil,
   On hill and plain
   True kings we'll reign,
The victors of the soil.
  But let the rash intruder dare
   To touch our darling strand,
     The martial fires
     That thrilled our sires
Would light him from the land.

Health smiles with rosy face
Amid our sunny dales,
   And torrents strong
   Fling hymn and song
Through all the mossy vales;
Our sons are living men,
Our daughters fond and fair;
   A thousand isles
   Where Plenty smiles,
Make glad the brow of Care.
  But let the rash intruder dare
   To touch our darling strand,
     The martial fires
     That thrilled our sires
Would flame throughout the land.

And if in future years
One wretch should turn and fly,
   Let weeping Fame
   Blot out his name
From Freedom's hallowed sky;
Or should our sons e'er prove
A coward, traitor race,--
   Just heaven! frown
   In thunder down,
T'avenge the foul disgrace!
  But let the rash intruder dare
   To touch our darling strand,
    The martial fires
    That thrilled our sires
Would light him from the land.

THE SLEIGH-BELL

McDonnell, John F.

The eve is clear, and the golden light
Plays on the Winter's robe of white.
Smooth is the road on the dazzling snow,
Lightly the sleighs o'er the deep drifts go:--
Ours is a path as wild and free
As a bounding bark's on the stormy sea.
The sleigh-bells chime on the frosty air,
Like the voice of a spirit chanting there,
They joys of the Winter's festive hour,
Though it brings not fruit, nor blooming flower.
   Tinkle, tinkle!--the sleigh-bells' chime
    Mounts on the wings of the frosty air,
   Like the song of a bird of a summer clime,
    When the woods are green, and the sky is fair.

Over hill and plain, we swiftly glide,--
O'er the ice-bound river's foaming tide,
And deep in the vale where the dark pine trees
Shelter our path from the biting breeze.
The Eve is fading,--the pall of Night
Closeth the East from our straining sight,
And far in the West, a dying glow
Throws a crimson blush o'er the sea of snow
Then speed us on, for the sun is set;
Through the forest's gloom, we've a long way yet.
   Tinkle, tinkle!--the sleigh bells' chime
    Rings through the forest vales afar,
  And from the dome of heaven's bright clime,
    Glimmers the ray of the Evening Star

FROST ON THE WINDOW

Faulkner, Rhoda A., Mrs.

There's not a thing that Nature's hand hath made,
However simple be its outward seeming,
To careless eye or listless ear displayed,
    But hath a hidden meaning.

Alike, unto the Saint's or Atheist's ear
The anthem of the woodland choir is given;
One hears "the lark," what doth the other hear?
    A hymn of praise to heaven.

The glowing rainbow steals its silent march
Athwart the sky when rain-drops gem the sod,
One sees three gorgeous hues in Heaven's arch,
    And one--the law of God.

The winter moon was shining coldly bright:
The birds and leaves had left the trees together,
Save here and there, one, that on some lone height
    Still braved the bitter weather.

And o'er the window crept the hoary frost,
With many a wayward freak and curious antic,
In varied lines, that quaintly blent and crossed
    In tracery romantic.

Here, bloomed a wreath of pure pale flowers,
As hueless as the faded cheek of death;
There, rose tall pinnacles and Gothic towers,
    That melted with a breath.

And trees and foliage rich--the dinted oak,
The willow, wan and still, like settled grief,
The hazel, easy bent, but hardly broke,
    And varying maple leaf--

--That changes still its green or crimson hue
With every season, autumn, spring or summer,
A sycophant which wears a livery new,
    To welcome each new comer.

The gentle moonbeam kissed the silvery pane
With a most sister-like and chaste caress,
As if it fain a fellowship would claim,
    With such pure loveliness.

And still more beautiful, the magic ray
Made all it rested on, leaf, flower and tree,
And lingered there, like innocence at play
    With stainless purity.

Oh beautiful it was to watch them there,
Those varied forms, so gracefully fantastic,
The handiwork, so delicately fair,
    Of Nature's fingers plastic.

And as I gazed, methought such sights were given
Not to our gross material senses solely,
But to the soul, like messengers from Heaven,
    Prompting pure thoughts and holy.

There's not a thing that Nature's hand hath made,
However simple be its outward seeming,
To careless eye or listless ear displayed,
    But hath a hidden meaning.

THE HURON CAROL
St. Jean de Brebuef 1640's

'Twas in the moon of winter time,
0 when all the birds had fled,
that mighty Gitchi-Manitou
sent angel choirs instead;
before their light the stars grew dim,
and wondering hunters heard the hymn:
Jesus your King is born, Jesus is born,
in excelsis gloria.

Within a lodge of broken bark
the tender babe was found,
a ragged robe of rabbit skin
enwrapped his beauty round;
but as the hunter braves drew nigh,
the angel song rang loud and high:
Jesus your King is born, Jesus is born,
in excelsis gloria.

INDIAN SUMMER, *Moodie, Susanna (1803-1885)*

By the purple haze that lies
  On the distant rocky heights,
By the deep blue of the skies,
  By the smoky amber light,
Through the forest arches streaming
Where Nature on her throne sits dreaming,
And the sun is scarcely gleaming,
  Through the cloudlets, snowy white,--
Winter's lovely herald greets us,
Ere the ice-crowned tyrant meets us--

A mellow softness fills the air,--
  No breeze on wanton wing steals by,
To break the holy quiet there,
  Or makes the waters fret and sigh,
Or the golden alders shiver,
That bend to kiss the placid river,
Flowing on, and on forever,
  But the little waves are sleeping,
  O'er the pebbles slowly creeping,
  That last night were flashing, leaping,
Driven by the restless breeze,
In lines of foam beneath yon trees--

Dressed in robes of gorgeous hue,
  Brown and gold with crimson blent;
The forest to the waters blue
  Its own enchanting tints has lent;--
In their dark depths, life-like glowing,
We see a second forest growing,
Each pictured leaf and branch bestowing
A fairy grace to that twin wood,
Mirror'd within the crystal flood.
'Tis pleasant now in forest shades;--
  The Indian hunter strings his bow,
To track through dark entangling glades

The antler'd deer and bounding doe,--
  Or launch at night the birch canoe,
To spear the finny tribes that dwell,
On sandy bank in weedy cell,
Or pool the fisher knows right well--
Seen by the red and vivid glow
Of pine-torch at his vessel's bow.
This dreamy Indian-summer day,
  Attunes the soul to tender sadness;
We love--but joy not in the ray--
  It is not Summer's fervid gladness,
But a melancholy glory
  Hovering softly round decay,
  Like swan that sings her own sad story,
Ere she floats in death away.

The day declines, what splendid dyes,
  In fleckered waves of crimson drive,
Float o'er the saffron sea that lies
  Glowing within the western heaven!
  O it is a peerless even!
See the broad red sun has set,
But his rays are quivering yet
Through Nature's veil of violet,--
  Streaming bright o'er lake and hill;
  But earth and forest lie so still,
  It sendeth to the heart a chill,
We start to check the rising tear,
'Tis beauty sleeping on her bier —

Early Canadian Poets and a Selection of Canadian Content Poems:

Robert Hayman (c. 1575-1629)
"The Pleasant Life in Newfoundland"
Joseph Stansbury (c. 1742-1809) "To Cordelia"
Standish O'Grady (1793-1841) "The Emigrant"

Poets and Poetry before Confederation to World War I (1850-1918)

Charles Sangster (1822-1893)
"The St. Lawrence and the Saguenay",
"The Hesperus"
Duncan Campbell Scott (1862-1947)
"The Forsaken",
"The Onandaga Madonna",
"On the Way to the Mission"

Sir Charles G.D. Roberts (1860-1943)
"The Potatoe Harvest", "The Skater"
Archibald Lampman (1861-1899)
"Winter Evening", "A Thunderstorm"
Bliss Carman (1861-1929)
"Low Tide on Grand Pre",
"Lord of my Heart's Elation",
"Morning in the Hills"
Wilfred Campbell (1858-1918)
"Indian Summer", "The Winter Lakes"
Pauline Johnson (1861-1913) "Marshlands"

Isabella Valancy Crawford (1850-1887)
"Malcolm's Katie", "Said the Canoe"
John McRae (1872-1918) "In Flanders Fields"

Poetry during the period of the World Wars (1919-1945)

E.J. Pratt (1882-1964)
"Brebeuf and His Brethren", "The Titanic",
"Toward the Last Spike"
Marjorie Pickthall (1833-1922)
"Pere Lalemant",
"Two Souls" (a letter from Pere Jogues)
F.R. Scott (1899-1985)
"The Canadian Authors Meet"
Robert Service (1874-1958)
"The Cremation of Sam McGee"
"The Shooting of Dan McGrew"

CANADIAN PAINTERS

I am indebted to Mr. Dennis Reid, Professor at the University of Toronto, and author of *A Concise History of Canadian Painting*, for providing this list of Canada's most significant painters from the early missionaries and settlers through to the Group of Seven and contemporaries. Listed here are some resources for further information on Canadian artists.

A Concise History of Canadian Painting
by Dennis Reid

Painting in Canada by J. Russel Harper

Virtual Museum of Canada
This site www.virtualmuseum.ca is a federal website that is a virtual tour of the museums of Canada. The works of Canadian painters through history in museums in Canada can be viewed at this site under the heading "image gallery." Many of the paintings by these artists are representations of historical events in Canadian history.

Using the book *A Concise History of Canadian Painting*, images may be found to use when studying a particular event or person. The "virtual museum" is a good supplement to find larger images of paintings that would complement study.

The Canadian Encyclopedia Online has an excellent tool for historical paintings to use with Canadian history studies.

In *Chapter Seven: Resources,* there is a description of of this tool.

The following list represents some of the most significant painters in Canadian history.

NEW FRANCE
L'Abbe Hugues Pommier
Frere Luc (Claude Francois)
Pierre Le Ber
Paul Beaucour

BRITISH NORTH AMERICA
William Berczy
Robert Field
George Theodore Berthon
Francois Beaucourt
Joseph legare
Antoine Plamandon
Robert Todd
Cornelius Krieghoff
Paul Kane
W.G.R. Hind
Daniel Fowler

CONFEDERATION ERA PAINTERS
Allan Edson
F.M. Bell-Smith
John Fraser
Lucius O'Brien
F.A. Verner

THE ACADEMIC TRADITION
Napoleon Bourassa
William Brymner
Robert Harris
Paul Peel
George Reid
Wm. Blair Bruce
Charles Huot

EARLY MODERNISTS
Homer Watson
Ozias Leduc
Marc-Aurele de Foy Suzor-Cote
Maurice Cullen
J.W. Morris
Adrien Hebert
David Milne
Emily Carr
John Lyman

GROUP OF SEVEN AND
CONTEMPORARIES
J.E.H. MacDonald
Arthur Lismer
F.H. Varley
A.Y. Jackson
F.H. Johnston
Lawren S. Harris
Frank Carmichael
Tom Thomson
A.J. Casson
Edwin Holgate
LeMoine FitzGerald

Chapter seven:
General Suggestions for Canadian Geography

GEOGRAPHY

It would be impossible to study Canadian History without studying geography. Here are a few resources that we have found helpful over the years.

Canadian Geography Flashcards (1) are a highly recommended resource for Canadian geography. Recommended over several grade levels, these cards are large, sturdy, laminated flashcards that have the visual aspects of Canadian geography on the front, and written facts on the back. Each province or territory is shown on a card, as well as a small map of Canada on each card that highlights the province and shows it in relation to the other provinces. Illustrations of the provincial flags are on the reverse, as well as capital cities, provincial emblems and highest elevation. There is other pertinent information, including the date a province or territory became part of Canada, population and area. Two additional cards show visually major mountain ranges and their elevations and major rivers and their lengths, and include informative text on the back. Canadian Geography Flashcards were developed by a homeschooling mother. Please see ordering information in Resources chapter.

Our Home and Native Land: Canada Geography (2) is an excellent workbook for learning Canadian geography. Beginning with basic geography skills, this book moves quickly to more advanced skills, making it suitable to use for middle grades. It encourages research skills. Inside the workbook is a beautifully illustrated binder sized Canadian map for children to take out for reference. There are many outline maps in Our Home and Native Land, requiring children to fill in different information, depending on the lesson. Simple hand drawn facsimiles of these or similar maps can be made and copied for review work, or write-on, wipe-off Canadian maps are available at most teaching supply stores.

While map skills are important, a mapping workbook is not a necessity, if the atlas you are using has an explanation on its usage. Most good atlases will provide this information. Typically in the front of a good atlas there will be a guide that shows different types of maps, such as political, economic or physical. The guide to an atlas should explain how to read the key to these maps, how to find information and location on maps, and explain different types of maps and their uses. Map skills are an essential aspect of geography and if you prefer a workbook approach, there are Canadian homeschool suppliers listed in the resources section. The skill of mapping is universal, and is best absorbed whenever a particular place in the world is being discussed. A good Canadian map should always be visible in the household.

LITERATURE TO STUDY GEOGRAPHY

Every book your family reads about Canadian history has a setting, and that should be used constantly to study geography. Children will learn innately how to use atlases and maps by regularly looking things up that they are reading about. A better understanding of the books they read will happen automatically if they understand where it takes place, what the surrounding area was like, how long the river was or how high the mountain range is, or other physical features that pertain to the story. There are a few books that are especially good to use to study geography; they are listed here.

Paddle to the Sea by Holling C. Holling: This is an engaging story of a young native boy who builds a toy canoe and sets it afloat in a river near his home. The story follows the journey of the canoe as it travels down the river and through all the Great Lakes. Through this beautifully written story children are introduced to an important aspect of Canadian geography.

River of Canada by Thomas Bredin: This book presents the history of the St. Lawrence and its influence on settlement and exploration in Canada.

The Kids Book of the Far North by Ann Love and Jane Drake: Including a section on the prehistoric Arctic and the impact of the Ice Age, this book discusses   stories and legends and the spirituality of the Northern people.

Into The Ice (see review under heading "St. Brendan and Vikings," in the general book list)

The Saint Lawrence by William Toye: The history of Canada written in terms of the great river. Describing the events and people in light of the importance the St. Lawrence had on the development of Canadian history. Many anecdotes and documents are quoted throughout the book, as well as the   use of maps to fill in details.

Farthest Shores (see review under heading "Western Exploration" in the general booklist)

Kids Book of Railways (see review under "Opening of the West" in the general book list)

Other titles in the "Kids Books" series are:

Canadian History
Canadian Geography
Canadian Exploration
Aboriginal People
Black Canadian History
Great Canadian Women
Canadian Firsts
Canada At War
Prime Ministers

http://www.kidscanpress.com/products/kids-book-canadian-history

http://www.kidscanpress.com/search-books?keywords=Canada

Chapter eight: Resources

All of the resource links listed in this book are on my website www.ohtthatssimple.com under "Great Books Resource Links" so that if you are reading a hard copy of this book, you can just tap the links without having to type them in. I can update them easily as new resources become available.

SUPPLIERS

A short selection of suppliers has been listed here, there are others carrying these same products in your area. All books listed in the literature list or elsewhere have been available through homeschool suppliers, local or interlibrary loans, or through booksellers online.

Canadian history timeline printable for a binder:
http://thecanadianhomeschooler.com/product/timeline-of-canada-to-confederation/

This link is a detailed Canadian history timeline:
http://www.lorenzeducationalpress.com/product.aspx?id=MP5133

Used booksellers online:
Alibris   www.alibris.com
ABEbooks   www.abebooks.com
Better World Books www.betterworldbooks.com

World Book encyclopedias and other products:
www.worldbookonline.com
    To purchase World Book products, click on World Book Store at this site.   A description is given of all of the WB products.

Canadian Flashcards
contact Laurie at ballycrochanfarm@gmail.com for ordering information.

WEB SITES

Using the world wide web at any time can open up an opportunity to expose evils to ourselves and our children. The internet can be an excellent tool, but should **always** be used with caution, and **never** without supervision.

Search for Canadian poets and authors through this federal website. www.nlc-bnc.ca

Canadian Poetry is an excellent resource, poets are listed by era. http://canadianpoetry.org

Virtual Museum is another federal website that features artists, all through history, their work, and where it is displayed in museums.

http://www.museevirtuel-virtualmuseum.ca

The Canadian Encyclopedia online has an excellent timeline, interactive games, quizzes and displays all about Canadian history. One of the features that I like best about this online encyclopedia is a section called "One Hundred Greatest Events in Canadian History." This is an interactive timeline, and when you click on each different event or person, a short paragraph about the topic appears, as well as an image. The images are often historical works of art depicting an historical event or person. It is a great overview of

139

history, as well as providing a visual anchor, like a timeline that you make.

All topics pertaining to Canadian history, like any good encyclopedia, are depicted with an image, but the images used on this particular site are well chosen, often historical paintings, and could be printed to go on a family timeline as well. This is an excellent visual tool.

www.thecanadianencyclopedia.com

Canadian Geographic Kids is a fun site to consider: www.canadiangeographic.ca/kids

There are some great general resources for Canadian homeschoolers now, I recommend checking all of these out:

http://thecanadianhomeschooler.com/history/

http://www.canadianhomeeducation.com

Contact information

Bonnie Landry
email address: ohthatssimple@gmail.com

Made in the USA
San Bernardino, CA
09 August 2016